Mushroom Growing:

Beginners Complete Guide to Growing Mushrooms at Home

Table of content

Introduction

Mushrooms are the fungal flowers and they are considered to be a great source of minerals, amino acids, carbohydrates, fats, vitamins, and proteins. Researchers have found them to be lowering cholesterol levels, reducing blood pressure, stimulating the immune system, and having anti-tumor properties. So, mushrooms are an amazing combination of both nutritional and medicinal benefits.

Mushrooms grow either epigeous or hypogeous i.e. below or above the ground. Naturally, they prefer to grow on dump places and manure heaps such as coastal and mountainous areas, plains, grassy grounds, bunds, manure heaps, water channels, forests, woods and fields. However, you can grow them in your home garden as well. They make a beautiful and nutritional addition in the landscape of your house.

For growing them at home, you need to take care of the environmental conditions and growing mediums. Mushrooms can be grown in compost, logs, sawdust and straws. Their growth process involves the steps of sterilization and pasteurization, inoculation, cultivation, and casing. Their harvesting periods are prolonged because of their short life spans which make the growers to keep plucking and harvesting the fruity parts of these fungi throughout period after casing.

You must identify the edible mushrooms from the non-edible ones. For that purpose, you need to know about the edible types. Let's read together!

Chapter 01: Edible Mushrooms in the World and Their Medicinal Properties

Mushrooms are the fruit bodies of several kinds of macrofungi. They grow either epigeous or hypogeous i.e. below or above the ground. Some of them are edible however the criteria of their edibility depend upon the presence or absence of poisonous substance in the body. This can be judged by its taste, aroma and poisonous effects on human body.

Edible mushrooms have both nutritional and medicinal values. They include various species of fungi that are either cultivated or harvested wild. Over 20 species of them can be easily cultivated and they are available in markets in over 60 countries as well but the difficult to obtain ones are collected by private gatherers. There are also certain kinds of these fungi that have neutral effects on some people while show toxic effects on others.

It is very much helpful if you can understand the interactions food makes to our body and the role played by it in healing various health conditions. Either you are using food as a prevention-focused diet or as a part of a medical treatment you need knowledge because it is the power.

There has been a widespread interest in the last two decades in maintaining good health by study the pertinent role played by the immunity system. Diseases such as AIDS/HIV, autoimmune conditions, hepatitis, chronic fatigue syndrome, and cancer occur due to immune system dysfunction. According to a scientific study, medicinal mushrooms are gaining wide attention from medical clinicians and researchers. More and more practitioners are looking to the medical effects of mushrooms on the immune system.

Shiitake (Lentinula edodes)

These mushrooms, native to Asia, have amazing antiviral activities and immune enhancing powers. They contribute to lower cholesterol. They also exhibit virus inhibiting effects.

http://i.istockimg.com/file_thumbview_approve/19172302/3/stock-photo-19172302-mushrooms-shiitake.jpg

They contain lentinan which strengthens the immune system. It is also believed to slow down tumor growth according to American Cancer Study. They also provide a good source of antioxidants and iron which reduce the damage caused by free radicals.

Reishi Mushroom (Lingzhi)

It is a Chinese mushroom. It is well known in China as "Herb of Spiritual Potency". It has powers to healing the tumors. It also lowers down cholesterol and blood sugar levels. It also helps with the balancing of the immune system. It also provides bacteriostasis and hepatoprotection in our bodies.

It has a 2000 years long journey in the pharmacy and that's why its nutritional values are taken over by its pharmaceutical values. This quality sets it apart from rest of the mushroom family. It can be taken in any form such as tea, dietary supplement and powder.

Lactarius Salmonicolor (Russulaceae)

It has potent medicinal benefits. It has antioxidant constituents, according to a scientific study. These have been detected by observing ten fatty acids and their esters in an extract of this rare mushroom by the researchers. The antioxidant activity was evaluated afterwards on these fatty acid and their esters.

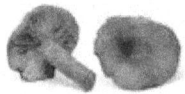

This antioxidant constituent helps the mushroom to contribute to the immune system's overall health. Thus it can serve as an anti-viral and anti-cancer advocate. This mushroom alone has 400 species that mostly grow in coniferous woods.

Coriolus Versicolor (Trametes versicolor)

This rare mushroom is commonly known as "Turkey Tail". It is very much used in most of the Asian herbal medicines. Two extracts from this rare kind polysaccharide-peptide (PSP) and polysaccharide K (PSK) are under evaluation by the American Cancer Society for cancer treatment.

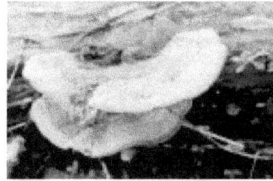

It is suggested by the study that PSK can help people to fight certain kind of cancers by lengthening the gaps without disease by increasing the survival rates without causing any kind of side effects. It boosts the immune system as well. It is used in the treatment of various HPV infections. According to scientific study women with breasts cancers can take advantage of Coriolus Versicolor mushroom therapy. It must be administered orally. It enhances natural killer activity and lymphocyte numbers. Remaining cancerous cells are killed by the increased NK cell counts. This helps raising the overall health of a woman with breast cancer after radiation therapy.

Morel (Morchella Esculenta)

This beautiful mushroom varies in shape, size and color and is rich in iron and vitamin D. Their flavor is earthy type. You have to identify the differences between the true and false morel due to their great similarity in color. False morels are poisonous. However, certain poisoning and allergic cases with true morels have also been documented.

http://images.freeimages.com/images/thumbs/380/morel-in-leaves-1327588.jpg

It is pertinent to take all the cautionary steps to collecting and consuming the right morels. They are abundant in immune boosting nutrients. Their health benefits keep contributing to the persuasive scientific research. The rate of these scientific studies has increased primarily in Korea, China, Japan and the U.S. in the recent two decades. But it is very important to take all of the precautionary steps to identify the edible mushrooms before utilizing them in nutritional diet or medical treatment.

The edibility of mushrooms is identified by proper identification and accurate determination. Otherwise they can cause certain allergic reactions and food poisoning in people. Great care must especially be taken in consuming these fungi for the first time and must be consumed in small quantities to identify the allergies.

Chapter 02: Supplies and Equipments to Grow Mushrooms

You will need some specific supplies and equipments to grow mushrooms at your home. Generally, these equipments and supplies are easy and cheap to come by. Growing mushrooms at home is not difficult at all. You do not need any kind of special knowledge, equipment and materials to grow them. Even the supplies are not expensive. They are fairly easy to be found. Simply gather the material and start growing your own organic delicious fungi with lots of nutritional as well as medicinal benefits. Here is a list of items with brief details that you are going to need in cultivating mushrooms at your home.

http://i.istockimg.com/file_thumbview_approve/46924544/3/stock-illustration-46924544-little-mushroomer.jpg

Spores or Mycelium:

Spores of an adult mushroom or mycelium of young mushrooms is the first thing that you are going to need in growing mushrooms. You can easily obtain it from a supply store or an active grower in the local town. You can also grow new baby mushrooms from the fresh, adult mushrooms as well.

Pressure Jars:

Next, you will need pressure cooker jars if you are not planning to grow them in beds. Take empty, clean jars.

Substrate Material:

Then, you are going to need some medium to grow mushrooms in. You have a number of choices such as straws, roll of toilet paper, corn, rye, woodchip, sawdust and compost. You can otherwise use an oak or cherry log. You can either use an old inoculated log or inoculate it yourself. The choice of medium depends upon the space that you can utilize to grow mushrooms and the variety of species that you want to grow in those mediums.

If you are growing shiitake mushrooms then a log is needed as they are best grown in them. For oysters, you can also use a roll of toilet papers if you are using a mushroom kit. There are a ton of kits and other artificial methods through which you can grow delicious mushrooms easily.

Containers:

If you are using straws as the medium then you will need to soak them in containers.

Plastic Bags:

Again, if you are using straws as the medium then you need to hold them with plastic bags or with reusable containers. You will also need elastic strings or bands to constrict the openings of the bags.

Scalpel:

You can also use a knife. It helps in detailed culture work.

Weed Sprayer:

Mushrooms require dumb and moist environments. You must use a spray bottle for watering your mushrooms as you don't want to thoroughly water it. Spraying increases the humidity level of the growing area.

Filter Material:

If you want to grow a good yielding mushroom species then you need filter materials such as cotton wools. They let the water drain out of the beds and absorb excess water in the pressure cooker jars.

Syringes:

If you are growing your mushrooms in a pressure cooker jar, then you will need syringes to water the growing mycelium inside the jars.

Disinfectants:

It is the process of inactivating the disease producing microorganisms. It usually involves the uses of ultraviolet light, heat and chemicals. You can also use bleach and alcohol for this purpose. You must wear face masks and cover your hands with sterilize gloves while doing so to protect your skin and health.

Thermometer:

Thermometers are used to check and keep an eye on the temperatures of the fungi and their surroundings. It is very important since you do not want to destroy your fungi by the avoidable variations in the temperatures.

Hygrometer:

It is used to monitor the relative humidity of the growing area. It is very important to use a properly functional hygrometer because the humidity is pertinent in the growth of the mushrooms.

Barrels:

You will need barrels or drums to put in the straws and other mediums for the purpose of sterilization or pasteurization of the medium to help your fungi grow faster and healthier.

Gas Burner:

You can also use an alcohol burner. It is used to heat the barrels to attain the purposes of sterilization and pasteurization.

Bleach Sprays:

You need to keep the beds (if you are growing the fungi in them) and the room or surroundings clean. This is to use to sterilize the growing room.

Items for Inoculation:

Latex or sterilize gloves and other items such as face mask, clean clothes, and spoons will be needed to look at the parts of the fungi during the process of inoculation.

Growing Area:

You need an area to grow mushrooms in which moisture is retained in the air. It is important to keep it shady enough and let some light enter in the area as well. You may also need some plastic sheeting to cover the area. It will reduce other undesired moulds and the humidity in the area will also be retained.

Chapter 03: Best Varieties of Mushrooms for Home Growers:

Mushrooms are considered to be a great source of minerals, amino acids, carbohydrates, fats, vitamins, and proteins. They are also referred to as fungal flowers. Naturally, mushrooms prefer to grow on dump places and manure heaps such as coastal and mountainous areas, plains, grassy grounds, bunds, manure heaps, water channels, forests, woods and fields. However, you can grow them at your home as well. Some of the best varieties for home growers are as under;

Agaricus Bisporus:

It is a group of three mushrooms i.e. Portobello, Crimini and White Button. They are different strains of the same species. White buttons are the most popular among all the three. It grows up to one inch to two. These are the widely available mushrooms throughout the world. Crimini is the brown button mushrooms. They are similar to the white buttons except that they have a more pronounced flavor and, of course, the color is different too.

http://i.istockimg.com/file_thumbview_approve/6355522/3/stock-photo-6355522-button-mushrooms.jpg

Portobello is the most impressive member of this group. They can produce brown caps upto six inches or more diameters. Their brown caps have a tender, meat like texture. They contain a woodsy flavor. They can live somewhat longer than the other members of this group i.e. seven to ten days.

Lentinula Edodes:

Most commonly known as shiitake, this king of mushroom is the most commonly and abundantly found type of edible fungi. It has thick, meaty texture. It grows brown caps of three to four inches diameter. It is consumed both fresh and dried up. It is also widely used for medicinal properties.

http://i.istockimg.com/file_thumbview_approve/4850409/3/stock-photo-4850409-mushrooms-shiitake.jpg

It has found by the researchers to be lowering cholesterol levels, reducing blood pressure, stimulating the immune system, and having anti-tumor properties. It is also been researched as a treatment to AIDS.

You can easily produce it indoor keeping the temperature in between 55 degrees to 75 degrees Fahrenheit. It produces fruits of about two to three pounds at two weeks interval over a period of two to three months. You can even vaccinate logs to grow them in the basements. You can store its fruits for upto two weeks.

Pleurotus:

Commonly known as oysters, these popular mushrooms look and taste somewhat like oysters. They prefer high humidity and if you want to have the best fruiting from this little plant then you must mist it two to three times a day.

They have further strains such as blue dolphin that contains a distinctive coloring and bears its fruits best at or below 65 degrees Fahrenheit, white oysters which is the easiest and fastest growing species among all the members, and golden oysters with luminous yellow caps that brightens up their color if grown in bright light.

Volvariella:

Commonly known as straw mushrooms, they grow best on paddy straws. They were identified as edibles and first time consumed by the Chinese. It is the third popular member of the whole mushroom family. They are consumed both in their fresh or dried form. Different industrial and agricultural straw waste can be used but they are best grown on paddy straws.

They are grown and cultivated in beds prepared in two ways i.e. chopped and unchopped straw beds. The last layer of the beds is covered with a polythene bags. When the small buttons or pinheads start to appear on the straws, these polythene bags must be chalked with the help of a blade. The bags must be removed then. It will facilitate further growth of the mushrooms.

Desert Mushrooms:

Many people think that this mushroom is a gift of heaven. They also consider rain to be its seed. In fact, it has a brown top on its cap that appears due to the presence of a large number of spores. These spores are used to spread seeds in the surrounding areas. Rain just waters it. It has nothing to do with the pollination of this mushroom.

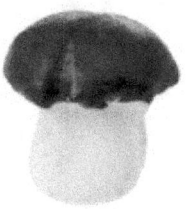

You can cultivate this mushroom at home artificially. No special tissues or artificially prepared spawns are required for this purpose. All you need is a collection of adult brown desert mushroom spores to grow and cultivate this fungus. The crop normally starts to appear in 30 to 40 days. You must sprinkle or spray water on the beds twice a day during this period of cultivation. The thread like roots will start growing from the spores. They then develop into small and milky like mushrooms. Just after two or three days, they transform into an average normal desert mushroom. Their growth depends on the environmental conditions as well.

Harvesting of Mushrooms:

You can simply pick them up with bare hands for harvesting. However, for the oyster mushroom you are going to use a sharp knife or blade. If your mushrooms have grown in thick patches then take extra care in cutting the grown, adult mushroom caps as you do not want to disturb the tiny, developing pinheads or mushroom caps in your garden bed.

You must also destroy or remove all kind of stalks and solid portions of the diseased or harvested mushrooms as this will decrease the attack of pests and diseases. Very less natural mushrooms like button, desert and black morel mushrooms are cultivated, gifted and eaten by people. Many artificially cultivated mushrooms are available in the market as well.

Chapter 04: Process to Grow Mushrooms (Light, Air, Growing Conditions, Pest Controls, etc.)

Growing mushrooms at home is trickier but not impossible. You can easily do it at your home. All you need is to control the environmental conditions as mushrooms prefer dump and moist climates for their growth. Let's read about the process to grow mushrooms;

http://i.istockimg.com/file_thumbview_approve/84096247/3/stock-photo-84096247-porcini-mushroom-group-in-white-isolated-background.jpg

Creating a Mushroom Growing Medium:

As per the growing medium, there are two basic types of mushrooms;

1.   The class of mushrooms that prefer compost medium.

2.   The class of mushrooms that prefer straw or woody medium.

Mushroom basically are fruits of plants which are made up of mycelium that is a thin, threadlike structure. Also they are saprophytic which means that they feed on dead plants because they do not contain any chlorophyll in their cells to produce their food by taking energy from sunlight and water and nutrients from the soil. They love to be grown in fiber filled environments.

Growing Mushrooms:

First thing first, you must know the types of mushrooms that you can grow in your home. You can grow them in climate controlled rooms on compost, also in darkened greenhouses on hay bales. Many of the people are also growing them on cut tree logs. These logs can be placed indoor or outdoor depending on the environmental conditions and needs of the type of the mushroom you are growing in it. All the types of cultivation of mushrooms have only one basic requirement and this is the provision of a controlled climate.

Compost:

The traditional method of making compost is to mix hay with animal manures. This compositing process allows the microorganisms inside the hay and animal manure to eat them and get prepared to be fed by the young mushrooms. The compositing material must be waters and turned every few days in the beginning of the process. Heat is released by the decomposition. This dissipates excess ammonia and thus the undesired microorganisms and pests are killed. And a uniform material is formed.

Logs:

Mushroom grown on logs such as shiitake are considered to be having better tastes. Therefore many people and farmers now prefer to grow them on logs now. However, this is highly favorable for the farmers with a continuous supply of logs. These logs must come from hardwood trees such as conifers, walnuts, sycamore, liquidambar, beech and oaks. Small logs mature the mushrooms more quickly. But the growth on the larger logs is sustained longer. Remember to keep high moisture content in the logs. Never let them dry out. Fresh cuts logs are less likely to have other or older fungi growing on them already therefore they are more nutritious than already cut logs. However, a log can grow mushrooms for several years if you don't let it get dried.

Sawdust and Straw:

Straws can be used in various formats. Their inexpensive cost and abundant supply makes them the most commonly medium for growing mushrooms. Button mushroom and shiitake are very well grown on straws. You can now even stuff plastic baggage and packaging to fill in straws and sawdust to grow mushrooms in them.

The Growth Process:

The growth process of mushrooms can be divided into the following steps:

Sterilization and Pasteurization:

The process of heating to destroy harmful bacteria in a substance is pasteurization. There comes a stage in the process of compositing that the temperature becomes high enough to pasteurize the harmful bacteria.

For other mediums, a stronger process is used and this is sterilization. It involves giving steam to destroy all kinds of bacteria even the helpful ones too.

Inoculation:

Spawn which is juvenile mycelium is used by farmers to grow mushrooms rather than using the adult spores. Inoculation is the process of stripping up the mycelium and mixing it up in the growing medium. Each piece then grows into an adult mushroom.

For inoculation while using logs, shallow holes are drilled in the log and filled with spawn. As a general rule of thumb, the more the spawn used, the more mycelium will transform into adult mushrooms.

Cultivation:

After the inoculation, it is the time to control the environment since the mushroom requires specifically humid environmental conditions to grow in. Controlled environments encourage higher mycelium growth. Increased carbon-dioxide levels and slightly cooler temperatures are maintained in the mushroom beds to yield the ultimate growth.

Casing:

Casing is the process of spreading a layer of organic material on the top of the growing mushrooms to enhance the growth level. Peat moss is the most commonly used organic material for this purpose. Leaf mold can also be used. The main purpose is to provide nutrients to the growing mushrooms. It provides a good launching area to form fruiting bodies. Casing is typically carried out in the case of button mushrooms.

Harvesting of Mushrooms:

On conventional beds mushroom start to grow in two to four weeks after casing. Logs and straw bales also produce mushrooms within a month after casing is done. It is pertinent to continuously harvest mushrooms as they start appearing on the top of whatever medium you are using. The reason is that their life span is not much longer and they die within a week to ten days after appearing on the surface of the medium they are growing in. Therefore, the harvesting process is to be kept continued throughout the growth months. You must keep the plucked fungi fruits in colder temperatures to decrease the deterioration process.

Chapter 05: Growing Timetable for Mushrooms

First thing to know about the growing timetable of mushrooms is that they grow throughout the year. However, fall is their favorite time period of the year and they yield plentiful in that season. Cultivated mushrooms are available throughout the year. However, wild mushrooms only appear above the ground in autumn. Exceptions exist in mushrooms too and that's why morels grow only in the colorful season of spring every year. This planet is abundant with different kinds of mushrooms but only some of them are edible. Eating others can be fatal for your body and can cause food poisoning as well. Therefore, it is pertinent to know as much about the fungi and their varieties before cultivating and consuming them at your home as you can because you know the rule, knowledge is power!

http://i.istockimg.com/file_thumbview_approve/5541894/3/stock-photo-5541894-orange-mushroom-from-the-amazon.jpg

Stalking the Wild Fungus

Mushrooms are found throughout the year. However, most of the edible fungus is found in wild forests in the beautiful seasons of spring and fall. You can find them growing in the decomposing wood or at the base of a tree. For harvesting in the season of fall, there are many kinds of the fungus that are popular among the harvesters such as Cantharellus cibarius (golden chanterelles), Boletus edulis (king boletes), and Tricholoma magnivelare (matsutakes). To harvest in the seasons of spring, Morchella esculenta (morels) are the best choice for the harvesters.

Therefore, before heading into the deep, dark, misty forest, decide what species of the fungus you are looking for because not all types are edible and poisonous ones can cause strong allergies and food poisoning in your body. There are many mycological societies that offer mushroom identification classes and mushroom walks during spring and fall in the jungle. You can also buy a mushroom identification guide or book. It is a must-read. Mushrooms are grown on public lands as well. And if you are planning to pluck some pinheads and buttons for you from there then you may need a permit to do so.

Growing Your Own Fungi:

If you are too thrilled to wait for any coming harvesting season then you can grow some delicious species of the fungi at your home as well. Also, if you don't like to take a chance on harvesting the fungi in the wild forests then home growing them is the best option for you. It is very easy and you can easily do it. You don't need any kind of special knowledge or rocket science to do so. All you need is to get a pre-inoculated spawn and provide it with the favorable environmental conditions and medium requirements to grow you the maximum buttons and pinheads at your home. If you cannot find a pre-inoculated spawn then simply take an oak or cherry log and drill it. You can simply inoculate it then.

Harbingers of Spring Season:

Morels are more plentiful in the seasons of spring every year. They have a spongy cap that is attached to the mycelium without any overhang. They are often grown at the bases of dead elm trees. Morels are considered delicacy therefore you need a special eye to identify the false morels from the original ones which comes from experience and maturity.

Harbingers of Fall Seasons:

Cantharellus cibarius (golden chanterelles), Boletus edulis (king boletes), Tricholoma magnivelare (matsutakes) and many other species of the edible fungi grow in the seasons of fall. You can easily find them in the wild forests or grow them in your home in respective mediums and controlled environmental conditions.

Seasonal Mushroom Calendar:

Check this table to know in what season and when can you exactly grow and harvest which kind of species of these fungi. It is the complete information guide in this regard.

Fungi	January	February	March	April	May	June
Sparassis	Available	Available	Available	Available	Available	Available
Parasol	-	-	-	-	-	-

Boletes	-	-	-	-	-	-
Lactaire	-	-	-	-	-	-
Mousseron	-	-	-	-	Available	Available
Truffles	Available	Available	-	-	-	-
Pied Bleu	Available	Available	Available	Available	Available	Available
Girolles	Available	-	-	-	-	Available
Morel	-	-	-	Available	Available	-
Porcini	-	-	-	-	-	Available
Chanterrelles	Available	Available	-	-	-	-

Fungi	July	August	September	October	November	December
Sparassis	Available	Available	Available	Available	Available	Available
Parasol	-	-	Available	Available	-	-
Boletes	-	-	Available	Available	Available	-
Lactaire	-	-	-	Available	Available	-
Mousseron	-	-	-	Available	-	-

Truffles	-	-	-	-	-	Available
Pied Bleu	Available	Available	Available	Available	Available	Available
Girolles	Available	Available	Available	Available	Available	Available
Morel	-	-	-	-	-	-
Porcini	-	-	Available	Available	-	-
Chanter-relles	-	-	-	-	Available	Available

Conclusion

Mushrooms are the fruity heads of some species of fungi. Some of them are poisonous while most of them are not only edible but they also contain many medicinal benefits. Therefore, apart from their beautiful, flashy colors, mushrooms are grown at home garden for many nutritional and medicinal benefits.

Many types of mushrooms such as oysters, button mushrooms and all kind of straw mushrooms are edible. They can be consumed either in fresh or dried form. They taste great and provide a number of health benefits such as they have amazing antiviral activities and immune enhancing powers. They also contribute to lower cholesterol. They exhibit virus inhibiting effects as well. However, it is pertinent to identify the edible mushrooms from the false ones before utilizing them in nutritional diet or medical treatment. Otherwise they can cause certain allergic reactions and food poisoning in people.

Many people grow mushrooms in their hobby gardens while others do it on commercials basis. Whatever the reason is, you must know the environmental conditions and medium requirements during the growth phase of the mushrooms. This really enhances the growth and yield rates. They are saprophytic and love to be grown in fiber filled environments. They make a beautiful and delicious addition in your home garden.

FREE Bonus Reminder

If you have not grabbed it yet, please go ahead and download your special bonus report *"Leptin Resistance. 21 Leptin Recipes For Weight Loss & Healthy Living"*.

Simply Click the Button Below

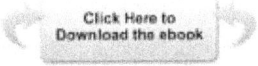

OR **Go to This Page**

http://easyweightlossway.com/free/

BONUS #2: More Free & Discounted Books

Do you want to receive more Free & Discounted Books?

We have a mailing list where we send out our new Books when they go free or with a discount on Kindle. Click on the link below to sign up for Free & Discount Book Promotions.

=> **Sign Up for Free & Discount Book Promotions** <=

OR Go to this URL

www.ingramcontent.com/pod-product-compliance
Lightning Source LLC
Chambersburg PA
CBHW072021290526
45787CB00013B/1719